This book belongs to:

....

CC—For my children. Always remember to celebrate who you are.
Reach for the stars, and never give up on your dreams.
Special thanks to my husband, family members, colleagues,
and students for inspiring me to persevere with this project.

First published in Australia in 2024 by:

Heartfelt Creations

 @ heartfelt.creations

 @ heartfelt_.creations

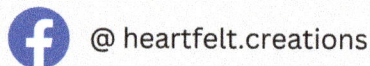

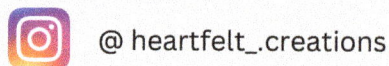

Paperback ISBN: 978-0-9756427-0-2

Hardback ISBN: 978-0-9756427-1-9

MY FAMILY

Created by Charmaine Clancy

Spot the Idioms

- An idiom is a group of words that, when used together, mean something different than the actual meanings of the individual words.

- In this story, the literal meanings of words in the idioms act as hidden clues, pointing the reader to the surprise ending.

Can you find these common terms in the story?

Flighty: To be very unreliable or irresponsible.

Sitting duck: A creature at risk of harm and without protection from danger.

The nest: The family home.

Ugly duckling: To be unsuccessful, different, or not fit into a group.

Bad egg: A dishonest, bad, or unreliable person.

Hard to swallow: When someone has said something that is hard to believe or accept.

Under their wing: A place where someone is protected and supported.

Jailbird: A person who has been in jail repeatedly or is still there.

Pecking order: Where people are ranked from lowest to highest.

Happy as a lark: To be very happy, delighted, or cheerful.

Talk turkey: Talking about something in an honest and serious manner.

Proud as a peacock: To be extremely proud of yourself or others.

Something to crow about: Something you're proud of that's worth discussing.

Like a duck to water: To do an activity and be naturally good at it.

Larked about: To have behaved in a silly or playful way.

Mother hen: To care for, worry about, or be protective over someone.

Eagle eye: The ability to watch carefully so no details are missed.

On a wing and prayer: To have high hopes but not much chance of success.

Parrot: To repeat or imitate what someone is saying.

Watching like a hawk: Closely watching someone, especially to see if they make a mistake or do something wrong.

Night owl: A person who likes to be awake late at night.

Fly off the handle: To unexpectedly become angry or to lose one's temper.

Rockin' robin: A lively and happy person who loves to sing and dance or someone who works hard to succeed.

Puffed up with pride: To be pleased or satisfied with something you or someone else has done.

Unlike most kids, I didn't grow up with my birth parents. They were **flighty** and wanted to travel. With no protection, I was like a **sitting duck**, so I left **the nest** to find a new home.

At first, I lived with Joe, a kind man whose job was to find me a permanent family. Others in his care wouldn't play with me. I felt like the **ugly duckling**, spending most of the day alone, although sometimes strangers came to see if I could fit into their lives.

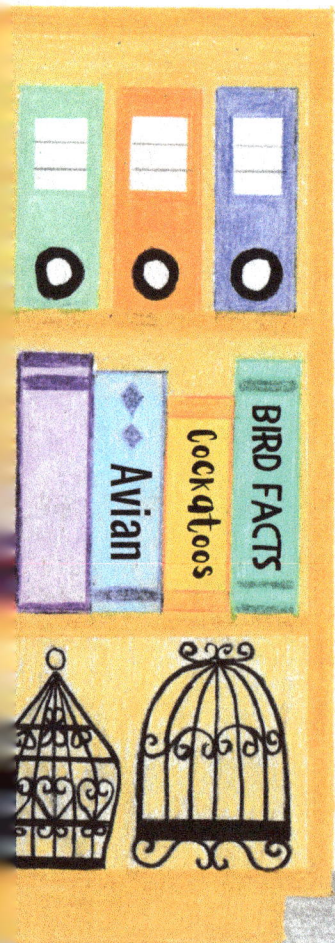

Over the years, my roommates found their forever homes. However, I only had temporary families because everyone complained about me.

"He's a **bad egg**!"
"He's too much work!"
"He has too many problems!"

This news was always **hard to swallow**.

Even though, at first, some foster families seemed caring and warm, I never truly felt loved.

I needed to find patient parents who would take me **under their wing**.

One day, a man and a woman asked Joe if they could adopt me, but he suggested they adopt a girl or wait for another boy.

I felt like a trapped **jailbird**!
Would I ever be first in the **pecking order**?

I was **happy as a lark** when the people insisted on being my family, even after Joe told them I was a handful.

Everyone **talked turkey** as they signed the paperwork, and I received a wonderful gift. My adoption was official, and I was as **proud as a peacock**.

We headed to the grocery store, and my new
parents bought so much food.
More than I'd eaten in my entire life!

To my surprise, they bought toys for me, too.
No one had ever been so generous with me.
It was **something to crow** about!

I just knew I had found my forever family.

We finally arrived at a house as big as a castle. I immediately felt at ease amongst the gorgeous flowers, leafy trees, and thick bushes in the garden.

My parents introduced me to their children, as well as four birds, three noisy dogs, and eleven playful, curious cats.

I was like a **duck to water** and quickly became everyone's friend. I was astonished that the cats, who **larked about**, were like **mother hens** to me.

Each child wanted to give me a name, so they wrote down Arthur, George, and Marvin and placed the choices into a hat...

George was chosen, and I loved it!

Since my arrival, every day has been an adventure. I enjoy playing hide and seek in the garden, and I have an **eagle eye** for spotting all the juicy and slippery worms.

My family treats me like a beautiful swan, even though I'm on a **wing and a prayer** to keep up with their activities.

In the summertime, while everyone else plays in the pool, I splash in the sprinkler with my rubber ducky, imagining that I'm a deep-sea diving emperor penguin.

Sometimes, when I try to join in with games, I feel unwanted and sad because the children grumble about me.

"Poor George. Poor, poor George!"
I **parrot** to myself.

I also feel different at night because I'm the only one frightened by unusual noises coming from outside.

I always see a boogie monster
watching me like a hawk
when I glance out the window.
I screech at the top of my lungs, and
Mum hurries into my room to comfort me.

"It's only a crow," she says.
"He's probably just saying hello.
He wants to be your friend."

I feel safe when Mum and I are
night owls together!

My behaviour problems haven't changed. Sometimes, when the children tease me, I steal and destroy their belongings.

Other times, I **fly off the handle** and chase them around the house until I bite them hard.

Mum reprimands me.
"George! Stop that right now! It's not nice!"

At the same time, she realises that I need time to calm down, so she puts me in another room and turns on the radio.

I'll often stay there for hours. I forget about my problems by dancing like a **rockin' robin**.

My family's love helps me to stay calm and refrain from biting. I was
puffed up with pride
when Mum called my former carer to tell him we were happier than ever!

Christmas is my favourite time of year, and the first one with this family was extra special. Mum taught me to whistle *Jingle Bells*, and Dad was so proud of me even though I was better at it than him!

I enjoyed playing with the tinsel, lights, and baubles on the tree and scaring my family by hiding under wrapping paper! But, most of all, I loved posing for photos.

We always laugh together while looking at the wonderful pictures in the family albums, so...

I truly feel part of the family.

I'm thankful that they love and accept me
just the way I am.

They class me as a son and a brother...

even though I'm just a cheeky bird!

I'm illustrated 15 times inside this book.
Can you go back and search for me?
Remember, I like to hide and to appear in photos!

All About Birds!

Ducks are water birds with a broad, flat bill. They have short legs and webbed feet. Compared to swans and geese, ducks are smaller and have shorter necks.

Swallows are small songbirds with slender pointed wings and a forked tail. Swallows feed on insects in their beaks while in flight.

Larks are small brown singing birds with long, pointed wings. They can be found all over the world.

Turkeys have a distinctive fan-shaped tail that contrasts with their bare head and neck. They're native to North America and are eaten at Christmas and Thanksgiving.

Peacocks are large birds that display their feathers like a fan. The male peacocks have green feathers with gold and blue eyespots, but females are mostly brown, white, or grey.

A crow is a large bird with black, glossy feathers all over its body. It has a heavy bill and makes a loud, harsh noise.

A hen is a female chicken. It can be found on farms that supply meat and eggs. It is important to cook chickens properly before eating them. You can boil or fry eggs and use them when baking.

An eagle is a large bird of prey with a massive hooked bill and wide wingspan. Eagles are known for their remarkable vision, physical strength, and soaring.

Swans glide on rivers and lakes in freshwater wetlands. They are known for their long necks and pure white feathers. However, black swans are also commonly found in Australia.

A rubber duck, or rubber ducky, is a popular floating bath toy. It is most commonly yellow and made from plastic or rubber.

Emperor penguins live in the Antarctic and are the largest species of penguin. They are black and white flightless birds known for orange and yellow patches on both sides of their necks.

A parrot is a tropical bird known for its brightly coloured feathers. Parrots are found in the wild and as pets. They can imitate and mimic the human voice.

A hawk is a large bird of prey with excellent eyesight and a long tail. It catches small birds and animals for food with its hooked beak and sharp claws.

An owl has a flat face, large round eyes, and a small, sharp beak. Owls are nocturnal, so they sleep through the day and actively hunt for small animals as food at night.

Robins are small birds found in Europe. They are known for their reddish-orange chest and brown back. The male robin has brighter coloured feathers than the female.

Hi, I'm George!

*I hope you've enjoyed the story based on
my life. Here are some fun facts about me...*

- Long-billed corellas learn whole sentences by mimicking those around them. This is how I learnt *Jingle Bells*. I have a wide vocabulary and have even said naughty words that I wasn't supposed to say. When the children teased me, Mum would pat me on her chest. She'd say, "Poor, poor George! Are they picking on you again?" I loved repeating, "Poor, poor George!"

- My wings get trimmed every month so I can't fly away and get lost. I also have a special ring around my ankle, which shows people that I have owners, just in case I escape! Due to these restrictions, I've learnt to run extremely fast. I also used to bite human ankles when I disliked someone or if they made me angry. Some say, "An eye for an eye!" Perhaps, in my case, it was an ankle for an ankle!

- Christmas is a special time in my house. Pets are treated as family members and get presents, too. My sister, Charmaine, pictured below, especially loves giving pet presents and plans to continue on the tradition! Some of my gifts (birdseed, bells, and ropes to climb) are illustrated in the story. Can you find these?

- I really was scared of the crows who waited by my window for meat scraps and bread. I puffed up my feathers and made crying noises, and my family would say, "Oh no! George, it's the boogie bird!"

- It's true that I love playing in the sprinkler! Here's what I look like after getting wet on a hot summer's day.

Charmaine Clancy (Author/Illustrator)

Charmaine Clancy is a mother, wife, and educator who has recently added author and illustrator to her job titles. Charmaine wrote *My Family* as an English class assignment in 2004. She based the text on her childhood experiences with her real pets, who she very much classed as family members. As time went on, developing the story evolved from just a hobby to a project that she wanted to share with the big wide world.

Charmaine places importance on celebrating children's uniqueness. She believes that while we all have different family structures and learning abilities, we can achieve our goals if we put our minds to it.

Now, Charmaine is on a mission to inspire people of all ages that it is never too late to write or illustrate stories. Whether they are published or treasured at home, Charmaine's motto is "Let creative minds be free."

Stacey Gittens (Creative Consultant)

Born in Australia, Stacey performed on screen and on stage before becoming a school teacher, children's author, and globetrotter. Now in the UK, Stacey and her children love to create beautiful and meaningful content through editing and designing. Stacey takes great pleasure when a simple adjustment has an impact. When reflecting on this book, she takes pride in the addition of idioms, bird facts, and Charmaine's dedication to perfecting illustrations. Check out Stacey's projects at www.FaithfulStories.com

Notes for Teachers and Caregivers

My Family complements individual and guided reading sessions at home and in school. Before, during, and after reading, encourage children to ask questions about the characters. This provides an opportunity to explore different family structures and discuss how to support the well-being of others.

Suggested activities:

1. Ask listeners to explore the character's feelings depicted in each illustration.
2. Role-play scenarios from the book so that children can practice promoting a positive mindset for everyone in the setting.
3. Discuss the difference between literal and figurative language, highlighting the idioms and similes used in the story as examples.
4. Identify the central theme in the book by discussing what acceptance means.

Aspects to cover:

- We should unconditionally love and embrace people for who they are, inside and out.
- We should be careful when using the word normal, especially in situations where people have a choice.
- We can celebrate the beauty of skin colours, cultural backgrounds, and differences in opinion by spending time with a variety of people.
- We shouldn't try to change people to suit our agenda, but we can always encourage everybody to be the best version of themselves.
- When people struggle, we can offer support by listening and responding rather than judging or quickly offering advice.
- We can make others happy by expressing ourselves and being true to who we are.
- Life would be boring if we were all the same.

www.ingramcontent.com/pod-product-compliance
Lightning Source LLC
Chambersburg PA
CBHW040316100426
42811CB00012B/1463